JOEL D

SMART COOKIES

WIT AND WISDOM FROM FORTUNE COOKIES
AROUND THE WORLD

ELEMENT

Boston, Massachusetts
• Shaftesbury, Dorset • Melbourne, Victoria

Text © Joel Delman 1999
Design, Jacket, Binding and Layout © Element Books, Inc. 1999

First published in the USA in 1999 by
Element Books, Inc. 160 North Washington Street, Boston MA 02114

Published in the UK in 1999 by
Element Books Limited, Shaftesbury, Dorset SP7 8BP

Published in Australia in 1999 by
Element Books and distributed by Penguin Australia Limited
487 Maroondah Highway, Ringwood, Victoria 3134

Cover design by Mark Slader
Design and typesetting by Penny Mills
Printed and bound in the United States by Courier Westford

British Library Cataloguing in Publication data available

Library of Congress Cataloging in Publication data
Delman, Joel.
   Smart Cookies : wit and wisdom from fortune cookies around the
world / Joel Delman. – 1st ed.
      p.   cm.
   ISBN 1–86204–494–5
   1. Aphorisms and apothegms.   2. Fortune cookies.   I. Title.
PN6271. D35   1999   98–37624
818' . 542028–dc21   CIP

ISBN 1 86204 494 5

INTRODUCTION

WHEN I was a kid growing up in New York, the Saturday night feast at the local Chinese restaurant was a long-standing family tradition. Lounging in the Lucky Dragon's high-backed red vinyl booths, playful pandas and merry peasants frolicking on the walls, was an exotic and adventurous outing I looked forward to each week.

Times change and people have learned that egg rolls and pepper steak hardly constitute authentic Chinese cuisine. These days, ordering a Pu Pu Platter may get you a strange look from the waiter. Dishes from the Hunan and Szechwan provinces have replaced the once ubiquitous

Cantonese fare, and smiling pandas seem as endangered on restaurant wallpaper as they are in the wild.

Still, one thing we can count on at the end of any Chinese meal is the bit of wisdom wrapped in cookie dough that accompanies the check. Though stories of their origin vary, there's little doubt that fortune cookies are a distinctly American creation. The crunchy cookie with the message inside seems to have been invented around 1920 by a Chinese baker in Los Angeles who handed them out as a way of tempting passersby into his shop; he may have been inspired by the Chinese custom of sending celebratory cake rolls containing birth announcements to friends. In any event, Chinese restaurants around the world soon adopted these cookies as a way to thank their customers.

While many of the fortunes I've collected over the

years fall into the uninspired ("You would make a good lawyer") or fancifully optimistic ("Your financial concerns are over") categories, a few manage to convey profound, humorous or remarkably clever messages. In their crisp, witty way, fortunes can offer real insight and guidance on life, love, success and happiness, their apparent simplicity often masking deeper meanings not always appreciated after stuffing oneself with Moo Shu Pork.

While these sage snippets are usually taken for granted and swept into the trash with their crumbled shells, I've been saving them since I was old enough to eat with chopsticks. One night, while sorting through my growing collection, the proverbial light bulb went off. Spread on the table before me were hundreds of bits of useful information, conveniently packaged for easy digestion in a world where many of us hardly have time to chew. No long-winded instructions for life or bland advice – just stimulating, often humorous bite-sized morsels of uncommon sense

Smart Cookies gathers the best fortunes from Chinese restaurants around the world in a handy, entertaining guide that you can crack open any time you need a little good advice, some food for thought, or a smile. There are even a few pages at the back for you to paste new fortunes. Enjoy them all, find your own favorites and remember one of mine: "We are each the architect of our own fortune."

Joel Delman
Chicago 1999

MANY THANKS to my agent, Laurie Harper, who truly made this book possible, my editor, Roberta Scimone, who from the start shared my vision on what it could become, my friend and fellow designer, Philip Golabuck, who contributed his considerable creativity to the project, and my wife, Mieke, who listens patiently to all my crazy ideas and shares my belief that a few of them are crazy enough to take a chance on.

He who is ashamed of asking
is afraid of learning.

The best chance for gain
comes through cooperation.

Truth is always the strongest argument.

Don't pursue happiness –
create it.

True courage is like a kite:
big winds raise it higher.

4

Don't be quick to change your mind
if you feel you are right.

When you expect your opponent to yield,
you must avoid hurting him.

Put up with small annoyances
to gain great results.

x

7

Do not mistake temptation
for opportunity.

*T*o be a man means constant revision
like correcting a writing.

Love is like war:
easy to begin but hard to stop.

Nothing in life is to be feared;
it is only to be understood.

What's vice today
may be virtue tomorrow.

12

Listen not to vain words of empty tongue.

He who gambles picks his own pocket.

Leave your boat
and travel on firm grounds.

Do not let great ambitions
overshadow small successes.

Confucius say:
show off always shown up in showdown.

It is better to be deceived by a friend
than to suspect him.

Delay a major purchase,
a better deal is coming!

Take care that your silence
does not signal consent.

Integrity has no need for rules.

Be careful:
do not overlook your own opportunity.

You will be wise
not to seek too much from others.

Enjoy what you have,
hope for what you lack.

Sweet memories
are the paradise of the mind.

Let your mind set in the groove
you think it should follow.

Mistakes are the stepping stones to success.

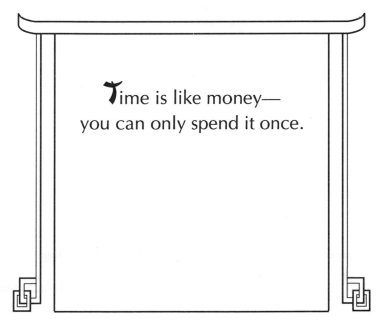

Time is like money—
you can only spend it once.

When you go out to buy,
don't show your silver.

Try not to stand on your own side
during an argument.

Water not only keeps a ship afloat;
it can also sink it.

Others need not lose for you to win.

An investment in knowledge
always pays good interest.

Hear with your ears
but listen with your heart.

Get off to a new start,
come out of your shell.

Stop searching forever,
happiness is just next to you.

It is better to be the hammer than the anvil.

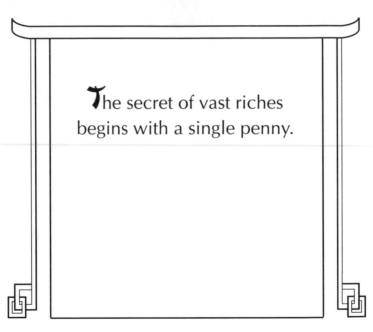

The secret of vast riches
begins with a single penny.

36

Move slow to judgment.
You'll be quick to truth.

Discontent is the first step
in the progress of a man or a nation.

The best prophet of the future
is the past.

Move from Me to We.

Fortune cookie says:
there are plenty of promises and hope
floating around you.

It is a simple task to make things complex,
but a complex task to make them simple.

It is better to lend a hand
than to lend sympathy.

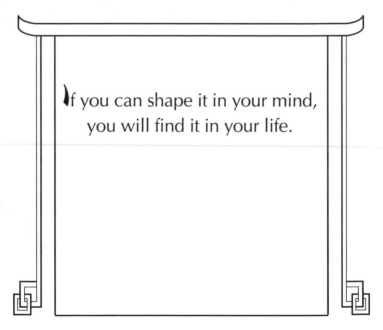

If you can shape it in your mind,
you will find it in your life.

Keep your face to the sun
and you will never see the shadows.

Some people never have anything
except ideas.

Be aware of
the Still Small Voice within you.

One who thinks first
will have good fortune.

Better to be eighty years young
than forty years old.

Rotten wood cannot be carved.

We must always have old memories
and young hopes.

Before you can score
you must first have a goal.

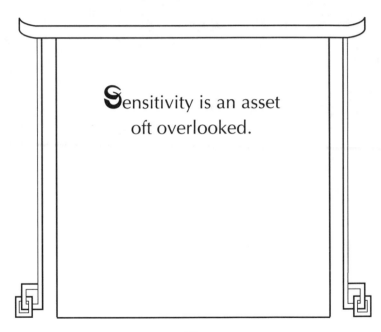

Sensitivity is an asset
oft overlooked.

How you greet a stranger tells more than the way you meet a friend.

Discover your companion's world.
Two worlds are richer than one.

A good evening is
one spent in good company.

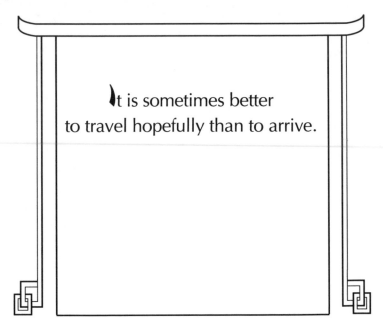

It is sometimes better
to travel hopefully than to arrive.

The trouble with resisting temptation
is that it may never come again.

One of the greatest labor-saving devices
of today is tomorrow.

Through eyes of love
all things take on new meaning.

59

Stiff in opinions,
always in the wrong.

People who are late are often happier than those who have to wait for them.

The best exercise for the heart
is to reach down and help someone up.

Idleness is the holiday of fools.

The end can often be found
in the beginning.

Truthful words are not always beautiful;
beautiful words are not always truthful.

Over the hill is much better than under it!

He who falls in love with himself
will have no rivals.

You cannot discover new oceans
unless you have the courage
to lose sight of the shore.

If you want a sure crop with a big yield,
sow wild oats.

$\mathfrak{A}$ new environment
can make all the difference in the world.

Don't fish for compliments,
you never really catch anything.

Being faithful to a trust
brings its own reward.

72

Answer just what your heart prompts you.

$\mathfrak{A}$ true friend walks in
when the rest of the world walks out.

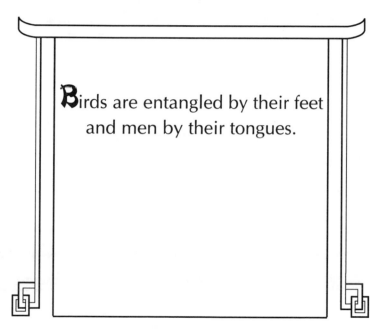

Birds are entangled by their feet
and men by their tongues.

Rest is a good thing
but boredom is its brother.

Ideas are like children:
there are none so wonderful as our own.

If all our wishes were gratified,
many of our dreams would be destroyed.

Walk with a good heart
and you will run with success.

A great man never ignores
the simplicity of a child.

Luck is what happens
when preparation meets opportunity.

The superior person is modest in speech but exceeds in action.

Over-deliver. Under-promise.

When you do something well,
repeat it often.

$\mathcal{T}$houghts are mirrored in your eyes,
keep them beautiful.

Be a smart cookie – look, listen and hear.

Anger begins with folly
and ends with regret.

87

You will make many changes
before settling satisfactorily.

There is never any harm in asking.

Love cannot be bought or stolen.
It can only be given away.

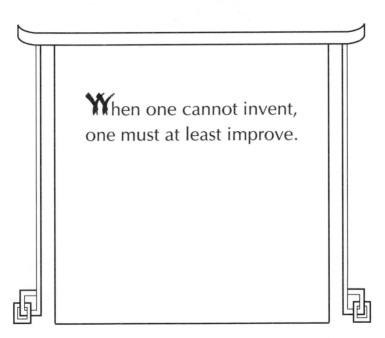

When one cannot invent,
one must at least improve.

Strong and bitter words
indicate a weak cause.

Inside every large problem
there is a small one trying to get out.

Work will always expand
to fill the time available.

He who has imagination without learning
has wings but no feet.

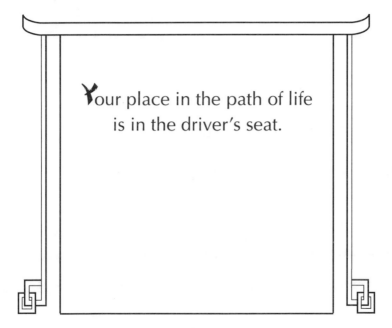

Your place in the path of life
is in the driver's seat.

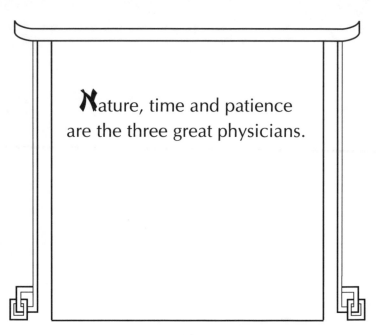

Nature, time and patience
are the three great physicians.

Confucius say:
person who laugh loud also cry hard.

If hand itches, you're going to get something.
If head itches you've got it.

Wise men change their minds
when they grow wiser.

99

Forget the doubts and fears
that creep into your heart.

*T*here is always time enough for courtesy.

A good neighbor neither looks down on you nor keeps up with you.

Do not compare yourself with others, there is no real comparison.

The best throw of the dice
is to throw them away.

Many small swings
bring down the biggest tree.

It is often better not to see an insult
than to avenge it.

The world is always ready to receive talent with open arms.

Your road to success
is still under construction.

From the garden of your dreams
many things can blossom.

A visit to a strange place
will bring you renewed perspective.

Don't bet against yourself, you may win.

It is up to you to create
your own adventures today!

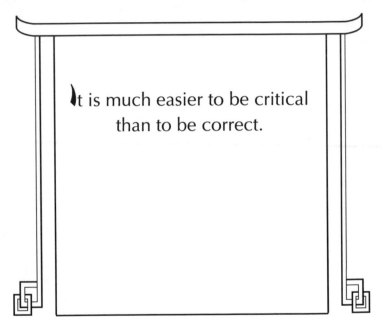

It is much easier to be critical
than to be correct.

A merry heart doeth good like a medicine.

How you look depends on where you go.

You are almost there.

Never trouble trouble
till trouble troubles you.

Even a blind dog
finds an acorn once in a while.

To one who waits, a moment seems a year.

What the eye does not see
the heart does not grieve.

The face of nature
reflects all of life's ups and downs.

A wise man knows everything;
a shrewd one, everybody.

Never remind someone
that you performed them a favor.

120

Stay on track –
curb a tendency to go off in all directions.

In jealousy there is more self-love than love.

He who makes no mistakes
does not usually make anything.

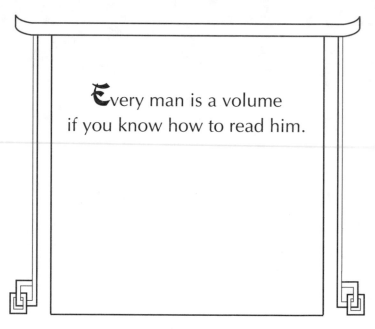

Every man is a volume
if you know how to read him.

Conscience:
that small voice that tells you
somebody's looking.

If you're not rejected
at least three times a week,
you're not really trying.

You cannot cross a chasm
in two small jumps.

If there is no luck,
how can we explain the success
of those we don't like?

Your problem is not a lack of ability,
but a lack of ambition.

Be both a speaker of words
and a doer of deeds.

As the purse is emptied,
the heart is filled.

You must learn day by day
to broaden your horizon.

A friend asks only for your time,
not your money.

Troubles are like babies.
They only grow by nursing.

Little acorns lead to might oaks.

Age can never hope to win you
while your heart is young.

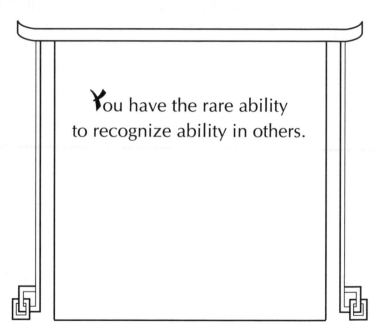

You have the rare ability
to recognize ability in others.

Keep true to the dreams of your youth.

It is always better to deal with problems
before they arise.

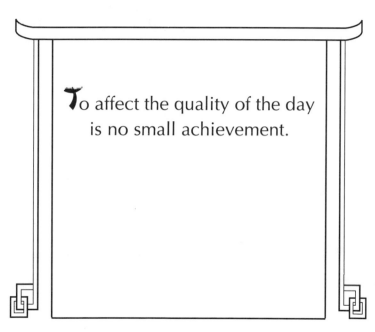

To affect the quality of the day
is no small achievement.

𝕬 liar is not believed
even though he tells the truth.

Of all the things you wear,
your expression is the most noticed.

You CAN have your cake and eat it too.

Don't hesitate to be demonstrative
with those you love.

If you continually give
you will continually have.

Don't let Monday ruin Sunday.

Joys are often the shadows cast by sorrows.

Be cautious in showing your true self
to strangers.

Cultivation of the mind
is as necessary as food to the body.

Behind an able man,
there are always other able men.

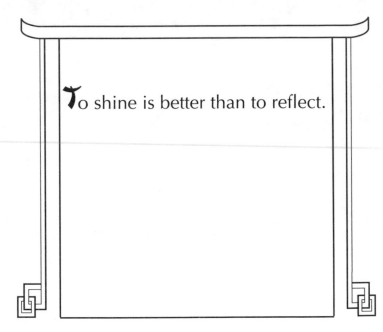

To shine is better than to reflect.

Share your happiness with others today.

Remember, every downhill has its uphill.

A phone call to a good friend
will ease your mind and lift your spirits.

A well-directed imagination
is the source of great deeds.

Simplicity and clarity
should be your theme in dress.

Don't force it, get a larger hammer.

A smile
is your passport into the hearts of others.

The worst failure is the failure to try.

Ignorance never settles a question.

People who expect nothing
will never be disappointed.

The more one knows,
the less one believes.

$\mathcal{B}$e direct,
usually one can accomplish more that way.

One learns most when teaching others.

A man who wants to lead the orchestra must turn his back on the crowd.

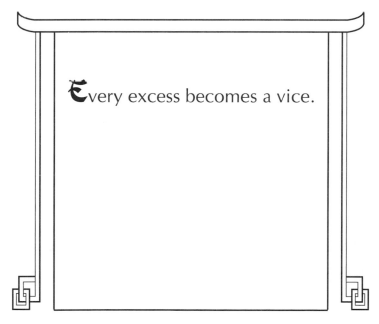

Every excess becomes a vice.

Speak only well of others
and you need never whisper.

Only those who attempt the absurd
can achieve the impossible.

One who is slow in making a promise
is the most faithful in the performance of it.

A useless life is an early death.

When in doubt,
let your instincts guide you.

The heart is wiser than the intellect.

A pound of pluck is worth a ton of luck.

The old believe everything,
the middle aged suspect everything
and the young know everything.

Your actions reveal your thoughts
more than you realize.

Optimism and confidence can cushion the bumps.

A close friend reveals a hidden talent.

See treasures where others see nothing.

Don't be afraid to take that big step.

Good to begin well, better to end well.

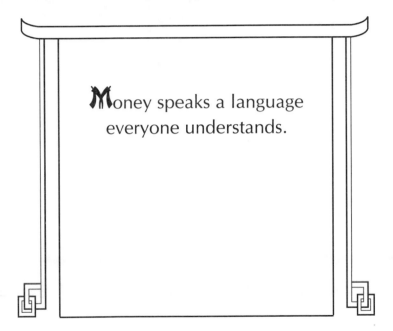

Money speaks a language
everyone understands.

Love truth and pardon error.

Those with perfect wisdom have few words.

He who waits to do a great deal all at once
will never do anything.

Though you are hungry,
it is better to have a hen tomorrow
than an egg today.

Keep your feet on the ground
when flattery surrounds you.

It's nice to be remembered,
but far cheaper to be forgotten.

The harder you work, the luckier you get.

Anything is possible with a willing heart.

You don't have to know where you're going to be heading in the right direction.

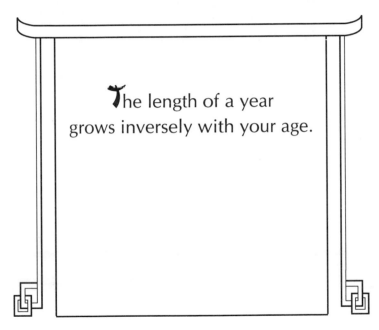

The length of a year
grows inversely with your age.

Many people with power become deaf and mute.

He who knows he has enough is rich.

Many a false step is made by standing still.

One can never know the best that is in him.

Look for new outlets
for your creative abilities.

Honor yourself
and others will honor you, too.

The great pleasure in life
is doing what people say you cannot do.

A small house will hold as much happiness as a large one.

Prejudice:
the child of ignorance
and the mother of hate.

187

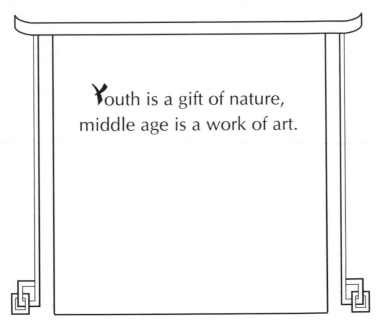

Youth is a gift of nature,
middle age is a work of art.

It is much more difficult to judge oneself
than to judge others.

7ime exists solely to prevent everything
from happening at once.

If it isn't your business,
don't make it be.

191

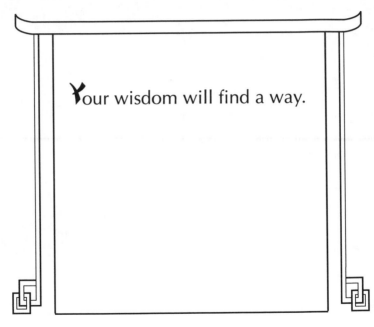

Your wisdom will find a way.

Learn to pause
or nothing worthwhile can catch up to you.

Great adventures await those who are willing
to turn the corner.

Revisit old friends, it has been far too long.

A smile can always overcome
the barrier of language.

Pray for what you want,
work for the things you need.

Live, think and act for today.
Tomorrow may be too late.

The will of the people is the best law.

He who expects no gratitude
is the most likely to receive it.

Don't first look for friends
when you need them.

Cleverness is serviceable for everything,
sufficient for nothing.

There is yet time enough
for you to take a different path.

There is beauty in simplicity.

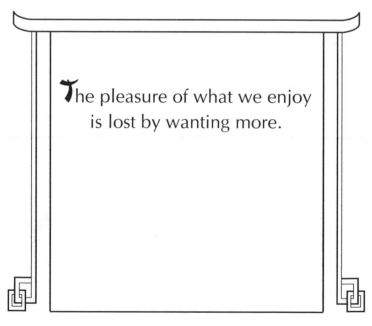

The pleasure of what we enjoy
is lost by wanting more.

Set your goals high
and you will always move forward.

Keep in close touch
with what your competition is doing.

Learn how to refuse favors,
this is a great and useful art.

Knowing and not doing
are equal to not knowing at all.

Build bridges, not walls.

Don't ever slam a door;
you might want to go back.

Be yourself and you will always be in fashion.

You can't solve problems for those who don't want their problems solved.

Look around:
happiness is trying to catch you!

Prosperity makes friends
and adversity tries them.

Money can build a house,
but it takes love to make it a home.

You cannot demonstrate an emotion
or prove an aspiration.

Wise men learn more from fools
than fools from the wise.

A single kind word
will keep one warm for years.

Boys will be boys,
and so will a lot of middle-aged men.

*T*hose who are always showered by attention
are seldom clean.

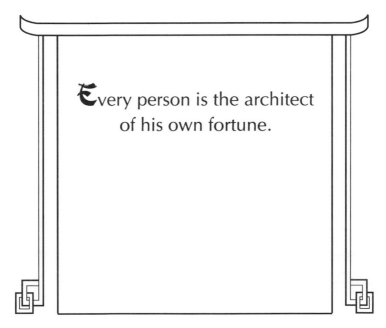

Every person is the architect
of his own fortune.

Being with loved ones
forms a basis for real security.

Bad excuses are worse than none.

Compromise in a dispute is rarely regretted.

Unusual experience will enrich your life.

Be careful! Bees with honey in their mouths have stings in their tails.

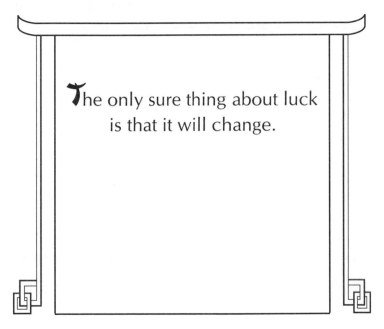

The only sure thing about luck
is that it will change.

From listening comes wisdom
and from speaking repentance.

224

Ask advice, but use your own common sense.

When writing is on the wall, read it.

$\mathcal{P}$eople who don't know where they're going
usually wind up somewhere else.

What you do with sincerity pays the greatest reward.

A truly accomplished man
need never talk of himself.

The climb is always hardest
near the summit.

Haste
does not bring success.

Never forget
that you are the guiding star
of someone's existence.

You always find something
the last place you look.

Learn to look below the surface,
beauty lies within.

If you wish to, you will have an opportunity.

To refuse praise is to seek praise twice.

As scarce as truth is,
the supply has always been
in excess of demand.

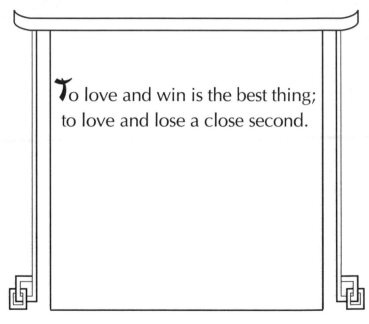

To love and win is the best thing;
to love and lose a close second.

He that has patience can have what he will.

A solid challenge
will bring forth your finest abilities.

If bargain hunting, be practical.

Simplicity of character
is the natural result of profound thought.

If at first you do succeed,
try to hide your astonishment.

Don't put off till tomorrow
what can be enjoyed today.

Stick to things as they are, distrust novelties.

Your first choice is always the wisest to follow.

Your ability for accomplishment
will follow with success.

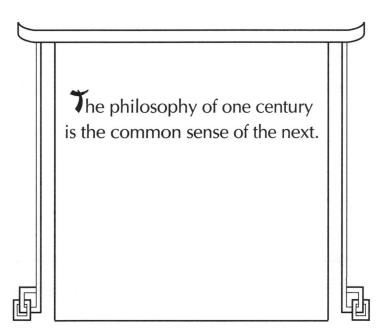

The philosophy of one century
is the common sense of the next.

Examine your actions today,
adjust them tomorrow.

He who laughs at himself
will never lack for laughter.

You have the ability to touch the lives of many people.

Meet new challenge with calm assurance.

Dreams and reality do not always mesh.

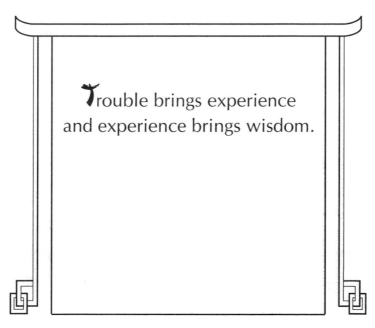

Trouble brings experience
and experience brings wisdom.

Bad habits are hard to break,
especially if you like them.

Old age is always 20 years older than you are.

249

Nothing in the world is accomplished
without passion.

Your intuition is excellent
but another viewpoint could be helpful.

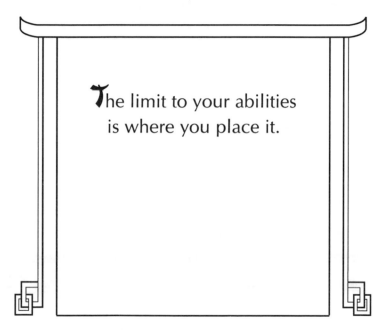

The limit to your abilities
is where you place it.

Apply yourself to the basics
and progress will follow.

There is no grief
which time does not lessen and soften.

Success in the end eclipses mistakes along the way.

Your example will inspire others.

Good company in a journey
makes the way seem shorter.

You can hire men to work for you,
but win their hearts
to have them work with you.

You can do anything you ought to.

Depart not from the path
which fate has you assigned.

One man tells a falsehood,
one hundred repeat it as true.

Let there be magic in your smile
and firmness in your handshake.

Success will come with patience.

Don't let friends impose on you.

Straight trees often have crooked roots.

Caution at first is better than tears later.

What's hidden in an empty box?

Absence sharpens love,
presence strengthens it.

264

Genius does what it must,
and talent does what it can.

It is the hope and dreams we have
that make us great.

Don't rush.
It is sometimes better
to take things one step at a time.

A fool at forty is a fool indeed.

Well arranged time
is a sign of a well arranged mind.

Be true to your honest beliefs to stay strong.

He that knows nothing doubts nothing.

A good laugh and a good cry
both cleanse the mind.

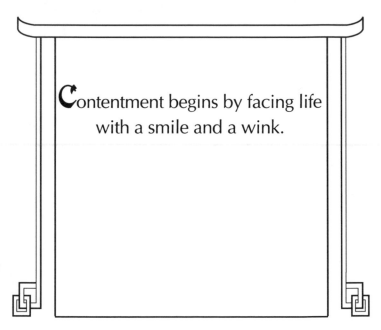

Contentment begins by facing life with a smile and a wink.

A man travels far in search of happiness
and returns home to find it.

There will be plenty of time to work hard;
enjoy yourself!

Pardon is the choicest flower of victory.

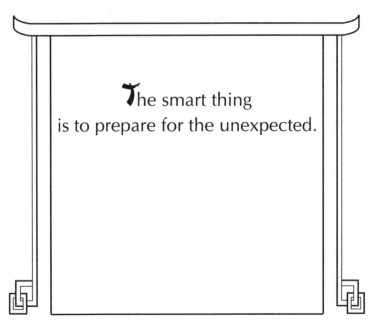

The smart thing
is to prepare for the unexpected.

Anything is possible
if you truly believe it to be.

Your mind is filled with new ideas.
Do not let them go to waste.

If you look in the right places,
you can find some good offerings.

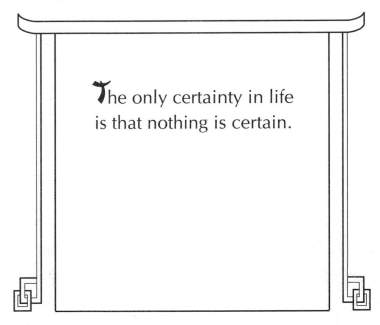

The only certainty in life
is that nothing is certain.

279

Many receive advice,
only the wise profit by it.

All the troubles you have
can pass away very quickly.

Life is a tragedy for those who feel
and a comedy for those who think.

Forgiveness is the balm
that heals all wounds.

Time is the wisest counselor.

Fortune knocks at least once
on every man's door. Be sure to answer!

Big journeys begin with a single step.

The crooked path is rarely the shortest.

Get your mind set –
confidence will lead you on.

Never postpone today
what cannot be done tomorrow.

He who knows does not speak;
he who speaks does not know.
– *Laotzu*

Procrastination is the thief of time,
but so is planning too far ahead.

The simplest answer is to act.

If walking on thin ice,
why not dance?

Save your favorite fortunes here.